CHARTERING SUCCESS

The Birth of Charter Schools in the Nation and a Rebirth and Look into DeKalb Academy of Technology and Environment Charter School, Inc.

MAURY WILLS, Ed.D.

CHARTERING SUCCESS

The Birth of Charter Schools in the Nation and a Rebirth and Look into DeKalb Academy of Technology and Environment Charter School, Inc.

MAURY WILLS, Ed.D.

LITHONIA, GA

Copyright 2019 – Maury Wills

No part of this publication may be reproduced, stored in a retrieval system or transmitted in any form or by any means, electronic, mechanical, photocopying, recording or otherwise, without the expressed written permission of the publisher.

Publisher:
MEWE, LLC
www.mewellc.com

First Edition
ISBN: 978-1-7324327-6-5

Library of Congress Control Number: 2019941749

Printed in the United States of America.

*This book is dedicated to my mother, father, brother, and grandparents, who have been my role models and have supported me unconditionally, with relentless encouragement and blessings. In addition, I would like to recognize my family members, who value education and have laid the foundation, and have influenced me throughout my educational journey to make a difference in the lives of so many children. You have always been my heroes and heroines.
For this, I salute you all!*

TABLE OF CONTENTS

Acknowledgments ix

Foreword.. xi

Preface xiii

Chapter 1 – The Inauguration of Charter Schools 1

Chapter 2 – School Choice Characteristics 15

Chapter 3 – History of DATE 31

Chapter 4 – What Really Matters in a Charter School 43

Chapter 5 – What the Data Reveals…..................................... 55

Chapter 6 – Putting the Pieces Together 69

About the Author 81

ACKNOWLEDGMENTS

I am truly honored to have gone through this journey, advancing not only my goals and aspirations, but being able to offer the support and encouragement to others, as I make a final destination of this journey in writing this book. As an advocate for children, I have always been steadfast in my commitment to service, high expectations, and standards. While completing this writing, I have realized that these words are not mine alone, but are echoed and resonated through the actions, voices, and even hopes for the stakeholders of the educational entity I serve.

I am also truly honored to have been a part of an outstanding and notable educational team, group of students, and electrifying environment, DeKalb Academy of Technology and Environment, Inc. This academy has provided me with the utmost support and stamina that have continued to guide and nourish, not only my mind, but my soul as well. For that, I say that I will forever be grateful and indebted.

As I close, I want to thank my Heavenly Father for blessing me with the tools of love, patience, and a conscience to mold and craft the young minds of children and change the world that they are in. My devotion to children and education has always been a priority and I want to thank the Lord for choosing me to be in a position, where I can truly make a difference in the lives of children.

FOREWORD

This book provides a glimpse into an amazing story of an educator with instructional leadership skills that brought together a community of learners to support high student achievement, using a Charter School's format. In *Chartering Success*, Dr. Wills examines the research in building a high achieving Charter School that can empower educators to achieve success in educating all children. This story engages the reader in a process that focuses on the success of students, who build high achieving schools. The author, Dr. Wills, wants us to keep in mind that "successful schools" can only be successful when students are learning and achieving their goals. He also wants to bring new meaning in how to translate beliefs and assumptions into practice.

Dr. Wills is the CEO of a STEM Charter School in Georgia and an outstanding advocate for student learning and the community surrounding those students. His instructional leadership is deeply rooted in his philosophy of excellence and learning; "Every student will learn, given the opportunity to embrace a climate of high expectations, a committed support system, and connections to the context of the real world, the Three R's: Learning with Relationships, Relevance, and Rigor!"

This book is an eye-opener to many of the questions community and educators have asked about choice and accountability. We can also experience the importance of early learning and how it translates to building a foundation for all future learning. The research sends a powerful message to educators, parents, community, and the business world. Children are at the center of all we do to achieve the quality of life that we so desperately seek. This is our call to action with practical suggestions and a framework for student learning.

It has been my great honor to introduce you to the author and share this message regarding his work and the many benefits to readers. I have had an opportunity to observe his work and dedication to student learning. He has "walked the walk and certainly qualified to "talk the talk."

Ida H. Love, Ph.D.
Education Advisor/Consultant
Superintendent of Schools,
Decatur City Schools
Deputy State Superintendent,
State of Georgia, Curriculum and Instruction

PREFACE

From early childhood, right through to our adulthood, we love to play with puzzles. Puzzles are also an important educational learning tool for toddlers and young children, as they provide many skills and mental learning benefits and opportunities. As we become adults, the art of puzzling develops many of the techniques we utilize to enhance and support our analytic thinking, creativity, level of awareness, and the effect of completeness, as well as wholeness.

As I began my educational career as a novice teacher, the academia world seemed to be a lot of little pieces that I needed to match in order to find a wholeness to the many entities of teaching, learning, and leadership skills that would soon develop my wholeness and fulfill my completeness as a transformational leader. This; however, did not come with only directions, but also with a road map of confidence, unlimited support, and a relentless desire to evolve into a productive and moral citizen and cautious being. But to understand my walk and direction in life, I have to center my story around the welcomed and unwelcomed pieces of the puzzle, starting from the bottom.

Early on, the pieces of my puzzle were laid out for me; however, they seemed to consist of not only ever ending journeys with the attributes of being a unique, energetic, and creative child, but also with one, who has experienced challenges. While trying to simulate into a different learning environment with individuals who did not look like me, I soon began to act out and have behavioral occurrences that would soon delay my academic promotion, starting in first grade. Yes, I was retained at an early age, not because of a lack of intellectual prowess, but because of my social immaturity. Perhaps, it was due to not having all the pieces together of the puzzle to get me where I needed to be. Yes, because of the lack of simulation and the desire to be seen and heard among a group of smart and other talented peers, such as myself, I deduced to acting out to get attention and gained immediate feedback. It did not help my self-esteem either, being that I had a speech impediment and had to take speech classes from a local university to gain confidence in speaking at an early age. You see, I was given some of the puzzle pieces, that of success, but did not know quite how to make them all fit into making it work for my regiment and my life. So, with these challenges at an early age, I was beginning to be a statistic of a male of color with a stigma attached. They all, meaning teachers, could see my potential, but did not know how to address the unknown and undesirable behavior I was exhibiting. And until this day, I am not even aware of the unknown that presented challenges yearly in my early childhood learning experiences, but the pieces were there.

With devoted parents, who clearly understood the pathway to educational success, being that they were also in the educational field as well, they began to continue to help me with putting the other pieces together and to recognize my potential. As I began to mature, I was removed from my current school, where I had been for four years and placed in a new learning environment, my home school, with similar and like students, where I could now assimilate, with ease and little adjustment time. Although this would be the perfect solution I thought, it wasn't. For now, my academic prowess was clearly evident by this new environment and was not recognized as an asset by my peers, but as a liability, especially in fourth grade, when my peers' perceptions of me were all that mattered at this impressionable time. It was during this time that I really began to act out with unquestionable behaviors that would bring my parents to the school almost weekly with multiple suspensions. You see, I still had the intellectual puzzle pieces of confidence, knowledge, and courage, but I was not accepted based on those attributes, but rather on being the center of attention as the class clown and a troublemaker through it all, those puzzle pieces of peer pressure and low self-confidence.

Sometimes, you need the assistance of others to help you with the puzzle pieces, when you quite can't make it fit. This is where my parents came in and discovered a solution: to skip me, from 4th grade to 6th grade. Could I do this? Would I be able to keep up? How could I make this transition with individuals who were positive and would benefit my educational experiences and opportunities, even at this early age? I would be forced to go to summer school, prior to that promotion and learn all I could about the fifth grade, that which I skipped. My summer was filled with 2 months of intense summer school, with one on one instruction over 9 months of 5th-grade material consolidated in 1/4 the time. I was determined!

This was my chance to be in control of fitting the piece together myself. I had to prove to all, especially to myself, that this was an opportunity, where I needed to believe in myself and not let myself down, especially my parents. I now had the puzzle pieces of responsibility and accountability.

Well, fast forward another year, as I successfully passed 6th grade, while being an honor student and continuing that path to success in elementary, middle school, and through high school, graduating with honors, being a member of the National Honor Society, being selected as the Drum Major of my high school band – one of the finest marching bands in Central Texas, and also graduating number 34 out of 345 and being accepted into numerous colleges, where I finally attended the prestigious Morehouse College and graduated.

As a boy and growing into my adolescent years and finally into an adult, I was always curious about my thinking processes. Due to my previous educational challenges, I desired to be a positive example to other children, who may have experienced what I went through. You see, I now began to see the entire picture of the puzzle I was creating and wanted to help other children find their own pieces to complete their total picture of success, self-love, and preservation. This is why the job of educating and taking on a new challenge of becoming a teacher was important in my life.

My career as an educator was purposeful and expedient. My first teaching career began as a substitute teacher and within one month, I was hired as a teacher's assistant and by the end of that same year, I had an interview with the Superintendent and was hired to become a classroom teacher. As I reflect back on that process of interviewing for that teaching position, I was still in the midst of taking educational courses to become certified as a public school teacher. During my interview, I was asked how I would teach reading, being novice and green behind the ears, I simply replied, "I am not sure; I have not had that course." To my surprise, the Superintendent just smiled and chuckled. I could only imagine what was going through his mind. Nonetheless, I got the job, without having a completed certification and even more, I had the Superintendent's grandson in my class that very first year. What a challenge and what pressure that would be. As I begin my tenure, I was the only African American male elementary teacher in my school and one of two in the district. After five years of teaching, I was interviewed for a principal position, where I first taught and was appointed by yet another Superintendent. At that time, I was the only African American male elementary principal for my district and would be one of two African American male principals for the entire next five years.

During my tenure in that district, I began to face challenges, such as reconfiguration of the school district and was encouraged to seek other educational advances elsewhere. Now, all of the pieces I thought I had were only not fitting, but rather dismal and chaotic. I soon felt as if all that I had worked for and accomplished would be shattered and forgotten. I still knew I had the potential and the gift to reach children's inner-voice, as well as inspire adults and mobilize parents. Little did I know that all that I had seen the entire ten years would prepare for the biggest challenge of my educational career-ever and the most promising thus far.

I had to recognize that although the pieces were not fitting the way they should, I still had all the pieces in my hand and also had to remember the strategies of how I got the picture to look the way it did, thus far – having creativity, vision, respect for others, taking risks, believing in myself, having faith, endurance, self-control, and yes, being a rebel at times – going back to my childhood. It is amazing how your attributes as a child that may not have helped you, can certainly be an asset as an adult when you know how to effectively and efficiently use them. Turning the pieces around to make them fit, I soon realized a strategy to use as I matured. It is not necessarily that the puzzle is not a good fit the way you have it, but simple adjustments and trying various attempts will reveal unintended positive results.

While continuing my journey as a leader and a visionary of a charter school, I was often reminded by the pieces of the puzzle that one has, and its relevance to shaping our lives. The uniqueness of the puzzle is that you may not get it right the first time, the second time, or even after multiple times, but if you have an idea of what the concluding picture is, you can continue to try and attempt a variety of fits, situations, or even scenarios. Don't put any of those pieces down, but desperately pick up another piece, because it could be that one piece that leads you to success and your dreams/ accomplishments. Remember, although completing the puzzle is one outcome, the ways in which you manipulate and strategize and view the different angles to create your total picture in life are the ultimate processes in which you learn, gather strength and become whole, the most amazing process you can undergo and evolve to become great.

Maury Wills, Ed.D., Headmaster
DeKalb Academy of Technology & Environment

"Innovation comes out of great human ingenuity and very personal passions."

~ Unknown

THE INAUGURATION OF CHARTER SCHOOLS

CHARTERING SUCCESS

If success is judged by parents and students voting with their feet, charter schools are in demand as these people are practically running to guarantee their children's admission into charter schools across the nation. Although it is premature to rest on this slim evidence without other indicators of success, such as student performance; parents and students are choosing charter schools for a variety of personal and situational reasons.

Many within the public and private school sectors have been asking the question, "Where do we stand?" They want to determine the potential of charter schools. Why? Because America's standards of education are always being critiqued. Essentially, being scrutinized is not a bad thing for the charter movement. It brings accountability, which results in competition.

Ray Budd is the person credited with coining the term "charter." He established the charter school movement on the belief that a school or community should be held accountable for creating a charter for itself. He believed these groups should be responsible for implementing plans for education that are best suited to their needs and serve the students better. However, Budd understood that for his concept to be realized, the charter schools had to be independent of the agony of bureaucracy. He gained needed support from Albert Shanker, (the former head of the American Federation of Teachers), who wrote a column in the *New York Times,* advocating for education reform using the charter movement. Shanker spoke for the Minneapolis Foundation at a local seminar concerning this concept.

Minnesota legislators were quite impressed by the concept of chartering after Shanker's speech. And so, they introduced a chartering Bill several months after the seminar.

THE INAGURATION OF CHARTER SCHOOLS

Unfortunately, the Bill was voted against twice. However, it was eventually adopted by the State legislature in 1991, and shortly after that, the first ever charter school in the entire state of Minnesota was established. That was the beginning of great things to come. From the time Minnesota implemented its first charter law, forty other states jumped on board and followed their lead in support of the charter movement.

The charter movement, initiated by Ray Budd, has changed the landscape of how education is perceived and administered in America forever. It has created a new type of school that gives teachers more responsibility for curricula and instruction. It also places a greater degree of responsibility on the students to achieve.

> Charter Schools provide an alternative education and provide families with the choice to strengthen educational opportunities.

Defining Charter Schools

It is apparent that the United States of America needs charter schools. Therefore, it is necessary for educators and policymakers to embrace the idea of charter schools. Those who understand that the primary focus of these schools is to improve the plight of underachieving students in the classrooms of America should give their full support to this concept.

What defines a "charter school?" How is it different from traditional schools? Do students learn more? Are students likely to achieve more in charter schools than in traditional schools? Parents, community members, educators, and others all asked these questions.

Compared to traditional schools, charter schools are

relatively new. Nevertheless, they have expanded in record numbers all across America. They are given several levels of independence from State Boards of Education and Local District Boards of Education through what is called a liability system, which takes the form of a renewable contractual agreement with an authorizing agent.

Clearly, reforming the educational system in this way is a plus for America. It makes room for more parental control, cultivates healthy competition, and raises the overall quality of the programs and services they provide. Included in these programs and services are effective school leaders, teachers, and the instructional program. They form a definitive structure that enables and ensures that the students' achievement and parental control/guidance is paramount.

> Parents, the communities, the business sector, and other individuals are the ones who found, govern, and operate charter schools.

Parents, the communities, the business sector, and other individuals are the ones who found, govern, and operate charter schools. They have a vested interest in their success and changing the integrity of their communities. Charter schools are 'hybrids' of public and private schools, where students' performances are regulated.

What is the purpose of the Charter schools?

- To fulfill specific goals, autonomy, and the formation of a specialized student population.
- To emphasize small environments with a student/teacher dynamic that is more focused, nurturing, and less distracting.

THE INAGURATION OF CHARTER SCHOOLS

- To create variety in charter schools: diverse education programs, and the manner in which the programs approach management, governance, finance, parental involvement, and personnel policies.

- To bridge achievement gaps and boost instructional autonomy through better educational opportunities and choices.

Education has always been an avenue for many low-income and low-performing African American children to break the cycle of poverty they face from day to day and generation to generation. Unfortunately, access to quality education for these children has often been a challenge.

However, they now have a viable alternative. Charter schools have gained popularity over the years with African American low-income families. They are different from traditional public schools in that they are run independently and can chart their own course in terms of teaching methods that are more customized to meet the needs of those who attend. The parents, teachers, community leaders, and those involved create a plan that is better tailored to the low income and underprivileged students who attend.

Although research is still ongoing as to the success of such schools, it is evident they continue to serve a large percentage of children in our communities well.

With the inception of charter schools, low-income African American families in our society now have a more adequate choice when it comes to educating their children than ever before.

With the many challenges in the public schools – crime,

violence, poor performance, and other major issues – middle-class African American parents also want to change the environment their children are in and to give them the opportunities to enhance their education. As a result, they have a keen interest in charter schools. They think it's a more favorable option in terms of solving some of the ills of the traditional public schools.

Many educators, community members, politicians, and parents strongly believe that having charter schools is the best way to go. Over the years, several middle-class parents, children and teachers have constantly advocated the dire need for charter schools in their areas and have laid the foundation for the promotion and maintenance of the charter movement platform.

Chartering is such an exceptional innovation that nearly 3,000 new schools have opened since the legislation was enacted in the '90s with the invaluable assistance of the parents, community leaders, and local school districts. These men and women saw the urgent need to revamp the current educational system that is failing many African American children.

The charter movement has led the fight for educational reform that is beneficial to low-income and low- performing children, as well as middle-class families. The goal is to create something new and *better*. Chartering is the foundation of an ever-increasing movement that challenges the traditional ideas of how children are educated in our public system and what it means to do so.

The chartering movement first started in Minnesota in the early '90s when the first charter school was opened. This was the beginning of new things in the educational system for schools that were underachieving. It sparked optimism and hope for the students, their families, and the communities.

THE INAGURATION OF CHARTER SCHOOLS

The following 20+ years were progressive, and by the year 2017, there were more than 6,900 charter schools in the United States of America and the District of Columbia. Over three million children were attending these schools. This was a major victory for the charter movement and the numbers continued to grow annually. Clearly, the charter movement has made significant progress. It has equipped its stakeholders to champion social, political, and economic progress in the United States.

Georgia Charter Schools

On April 19, 1993, history was made in the State of Georgia, when, for the first time, legislation was passed relating to public charter schools. Since then, 65 charter schools have been approved by Georgia's Boards of Education and the State Department of Education.

> ... parents can choose the schools they want their children to attend without having to face the financial burden of paying tuition fees.

In Georgia, the types of charter schools are distinct and separate. There are conversion, startup, LEA – Startup and State Chartered. By the end of the academic year in 2006, some forty-eight schools were in operation. However, there was a marked decrease since the legislation was enacted. Some 20,050 students are being taught in public charter schools in Georgia averaging 418 students per charter school (as opposed to the national average of 637 students per charter school).

Interestingly, although the number of charter schools in Georgia may have decreased, you will find that the enrollment of students in charter schools is on the increase. As a result,

Georgia charter schools have led the way in meeting state assessment benchmarks.

The charter schools in Georgia have done well in accomplishing this, as they were strategic in meeting the standards for State and Federal levels. These major achievements of the Georgia charter schools clearly demonstrate that the Georgia charter movement is critical to reforming education.

Summary

A lot of pressure is brought to bear on the American education system to produce students, who are literate and proficient in its public schools. Therefore, we must pay particular attention to and take a genuine interest in the process. Over the years, we have seen that charter schools have the potential to produce students, who are more progressive and challenging than those who attend traditional schools.

Every year, Georgia has to make compliance with the provisions of the Elementary Education Secondary Act. Considering the differences between low and high-performance students, this creates financial, pedagogical, and resource challenges for traditional public schools.

Charter schools are more attractive alternatives to traditional schools. Why? Because they give options to parents, who may otherwise not have them. In other words, parents can choose the schools they want their children to attend without having to face the financial burden of paying tuition fees. Some also suggest that the presence of these schools increases healthy competition among schools.

THE INAGURATION OF CHARTER SCHOOLS

Those who pushed for the establishment of charter schools did so on the premise that educators, who were creative and not burdened by the bureaucracy and mandates traditional public schools are faced with, could very well adapt to meet their students' needs consistently.

Of course, ideally, the charter schools should have been studied and analyzed to serve as models of exemplary school characteristics. Some time ago, a case study was done to determine the level of satisfaction the stakeholders had in the performance levels of a charter school based on the thoughts, opinions, and other data of its stakeholders. They hoped that other school districts would change the education process enough to receive insight and guidance on how to:

- Implement practical goals to attain satisfaction
- Carry out changes that will reap success for the stakeholders
- Encourage consistent support for the charter movement
- Embrace extraordinary measures that impact leadership student success and support, and parental involvement

The abovementioned were important in finding out how effective any attempts to produce success, in charter schools, were. In particular, those incorporating faculty and staff, parents and students.

Four pertinent questions have been asked about charter schools:

1. What level of satisfaction do students perceive they get at charter schools?
2. What level of satisfaction do parents, who have children

attending charter schools get?

3. How satisfied are the teachers employed by the charter school with the level of performance?

4. How satisfied are the stakeholders with the performance of the charter school?

The numbers speak for themselves. The measure of a school's success has been the scores its students achieved on various standardized tests for over 20 years. Also, millions of low-income and middle-income African American children have the opportunity to be educated in environments that are conducive to learning and have shown great improvement in their achievements. The overall success has been tremendous.

One of the major problems public schools face is the fact that they have to concentrate their efforts on addressing the systemic inequalities in the American education system for African American children. That's why it is so important that we diligently work on the strategies, models of reformation and other initiatives that can make a difference for African–American children to succeed. No child, regardless of class, color or creed should be left behind.

> The vision, mission, and objectives of the school must be to create change that will help all children improve academically, including African–American children.

The vision, mission, and objectives of the school must be to create change that will help all children improve academically, including African–American children. Public schools focus so much on the dilemmas the schools face, they have little or no time to look at these important strategies.

However, charter schools have been able to fill the gap for those, who want to see their children excel, but can't afford to do so financially. They have eliminated some of the bureaucracy that delays positive changes or, in some instances, prevent them from happening altogether.

The vision, mission, and objectives for a charter school have, so far, proven to be satisfactory. They evaluate all students using national and local standardized assessments. These evaluations assist in classifying students, who have possible learning disabilities, and also those who are meeting and exceeding the academic standards. In doing so, they can create programs and use teaching methods to help all students.

The charter movement has spread across the United States and has served as a catalyst for change. Parents and the public alike have quickly welcomed the improvements they brought to African American children.

Why have charter schools been so successful over the past 20 years? Unlike traditional schools, they are free from the bureaucratic monopoly, which governs the traditional school system. Charter schools are free to develop innovative and unique curricula that best meet the needs of the students they serve.

Research was done to determine how satisfied the students of an African American open-enrollment charter school in Stone Mountain, Georgia were. This was based on the curriculum, instruction, professional development, parental participation, and engagement. This research included all the stakeholders. They took part in interviews and various questionnaires were used to ascertain how efficient the school was. Those involved in this study, played a major role in the success of that particular charter school and to effect significant reform.

CHARTERING SUCCESS

The charter school in this book is located in a southeastern metropolitan area. The charter school's demographics consist of mainly African American families, who have decided to select the charter school as their child's primary education agency. The research and case study in the book reflect the perceptions of parents, students, teachers, and community members, with respect to how satisfied they are with the charter school.

This book also sought out to examine this level of satisfaction based on the school's goals. One purposeful question was examined, which guided the writings: Do charter school goals provide a framework to identify and measure stakeholder satisfaction? Additional questions were used to develop a theme from findings.

The case study design in this book relied on three research strategies to determine conclusions and findings. These three strategies included interviews, observations, and analyzing documents. A qualitative design was used to describe the voices, perceptions, and experiences of the participants.

The recurring themes that were found in this study included student-teacher engagement, teacher creativity development, participation of civic and values, teaching awareness of recycling, conservation, and protection of the environment; and the development of local political decision making. The conclusions, findings, and implications derived from an analysis of the data, which strongly relied on themes, found that it is certainly beneficial in mirroring and replicating not only successful charter schools, but also improving all public school entities.

*"The biggest risk is not taking any risk...
In a world that changing really quickly,
the only strategy that is guaranteed to fail
is not taking risks."*

~ Mark Zuckerberg

SCHOOL CHOICE CHARACTERISTICS

CHARTERING SUCCESS

School choice is a reform movement, whose ultimate objective is to give parents the right to choose which schools their children attend. In other words, it gives them viable alternatives to the traditional schools. With school choice, parents have opportunities to select private or public schools for their children's education. However, in spite of its benefits, the concept of school choice continues to have its fair share of controversy.

Private choice lets parents use government-funded vouchers to send their children to private schools. Giving parents and students this option is done in an attempt to address several concerns about parents' and students' rights, church-state separation, and the standards of public education.

Alternatively, parents can choose the public school option, which comes in varied forms. With this choice, they can transfer their children from traditionally low-performing public schools to better-performing public schools with higher standards.

Types of School Choice

There are various types of school choice designed to suit the needs of parents and students.

- *Intradistrict Choice:* Parents can choose schools from within the district and outside of district lines.

- *Charter Schools:* Public schools that are granted a charter by the local school district and LEA. Charter schools have a certain degree of independence and their curriculums are innovative. They also abide by a yearly charter.

- *Magnet Schools:* These public schools offer a

specific program of study or focus. Mainly, they are located in undesirable areas.

- *Voucher Plans:* Parents get to choose from selected schools that receive funding from the federal government.

- *Controlled Choice:* Families can choose selected schools, but cannot interfere with the district racial, socio-economic, and gender status.

The truth is for many years, parents and others have been frustrated and concerned about the educational system in America. As a result, the introduction of school reform was welcomed with open arms by millions of parents and children. It has become a workable alternative for parents, who are dissatisfied with public education and want better options for their children's education.

Parent choice is at the forefront of school reform with a large percentage of Americans giving it a thumb up. An associated poll conducted showed that more than 60% of respondents believe that parents should have the right to choose schools for their children.

The continual scrutiny and debates on public education are attempts to improve the present structure. This is necessary if all parents and children in America are to be treated fairly and given equal access to high standards of education. The fact is that Americans have lost faith in public schools. Furthermore, parents and education leaders are very concerned about the failing test scores, rising dropout rates, and decreasing literacy levels. As a matter of fact, there has been a steady decline in Americans' confidence over the last twenty years in these schools. For this reason, school choice is becoming increasingly popular.

Supporters of choice say that the competition between schools has led to school accountability. Consequently, school accountability gives individual schools the room to experiment with different educational approaches. They also say that it gives them the opportunity to design models that will help them find a way to work with their stakeholders. The ultimate benefit at the end of these exercises is that schools will change their one-size-fits-all education model and choose models of teaching that suit the needs of the students who attend those schools. Moreover, the mere fact that parents have the right to participate in the selection process increases their involvement with the school.

> The truth is for many years, parents and others have been frustrated and concerned about the educational system in America.

It is also felt that school choice helps low-performing and low-income students in ways that the traditional schools don't and perhaps, can't because of their structures. Howard Fuller, chairman of the Black Alliance for Educational Options and a supporter of school vouchers said, "The only people who are trapped in schools that don't work for them or their parents are the poor. We've got to create a way where the poorest parents have some of the options."

All over America, the truth remains that poor families, unlike the more affluent families, are unable to live in areas with good schools. Consequently, these children are placed at an immediate disadvantage. They end up in low performing schools with low standards. But, they have the right to equal opportunities in education just as any other children. Their financial status should never determine the quality of their education. This means the gap has to be bridged and what better way to do so than by school choice? Two recent studies have found that choice programs have impacted positively on low-income families. Children, who had no hope of getting a good quality education are able to do so because of the advocacy of the school reform movement.

Opponents were also concerned about the potential loss of financial support for failing schools. They figured that if students move from a failing school in one district to a school in another district, the original district would find itself in a predicament, where the school loses essential per-student funding. Therefore, the loss of funding at the district level would be detrimental to the already struggling school.

Some opponents of school choice also have challenges believing it can, indeed, be implemented successfully, particularly in an urban system, contending that a student's move from one failing school will not guarantee a safe landing somewhere else.

Nevertheless, in spite of the skepticism, those who promote school choice have claimed a major victory in recent times. In June 2002, the U.S. Supreme Court held that a state-enacted voucher program in Cleveland did not violate the U.S. Constitution's prohibition against government establishment of religion. In addition, the passage of the "No Child Left Behind" Act of 2001 officially introduced public school choice into federal law.

The regulation allowed parents, who have children, enrolled in a school identified as one needing improvement, to transfer that child to a better-performing public school or public charter school.

In addition to that victory, the federal government awarded

$1.3 million in grants to three pro-voucher education organizations that would go towards disseminating more information to the public about the provisions they have in the law.

Over the years, public school choice has gained immense popularity at the state level. More than 6,000 charter schools are in operation in the United States. Debates continue to rage on about the merits of private school choice. However, some researchers are convinced that because it is now so ingrained in the psyche of American public education, it is here to stay.

In fact, many are suggesting that instead of debating the obvious that public school choice is advantageous, our energies would be better spent trying to see how it can be employed effectively through adequate funding and targeting of efforts.

Charter School Movement

The charter school movement grew out of a dire need to see radical changes in the traditional school system that was failing underprivileged children. It started with collective reform expressions that included alternative schools, site-based management, magnet schools, public school choice, privatization, and community-parental empowerment.

Besides the onset of charter schools in Minnesota, Philadelphia took the bold step and initiated charter models of schools within schools calling them "charters." This was done in that state even without the approval of a vast majority of educators and parents. It was the small percentage of reformers, who started that drive. Many of the schools within a school were offering its constituents something that was non-existent before the charter – choice. This was done with the two concepts of autonomy and innovative methods of teaching. Autonomy was achieved by obtaining waivers from many of the procedural requirements of public schools.

However, it was not a free ride for those advocating for "charter" schools. They had to show their worth and produce results superior to non-charter schools. And they did. However, over the years, you will find that charter schools were seldom closed for poor academic performance.

The ideal model of a charter school is one that is legally and financially independent. It has no tuition, religious affiliation, or selective student admissions. Essentially, charter schools are supposed to be run like private businesses, which are free from many state laws and district regulations. Their main focus and accountability are on getting good results, not focusing on processes or inputs.

There is some variation in the length of time charters are granted. Generally, it is 3-5 years. During this time, the charter schools are supposed to give an account of their performance and effectiveness to their sponsor from a Local School Board, State Education Agency, University, or other entity. This is done with the intention to help the school produce positive academic results and adhere to the charter contract.

> The ideal model of a charter school is one that is legally and financially independent. It has no tuition, religious affiliation, or selective student admissions.

Defining Charter Schools

There are varied and unique types of charter schools. These are known as State Charter Schools, Local Education Agency (LEA) Charter Schools, Start-Up Charter Schools, and Conversion Charter Schools.

CHARTERING SUCCESS

A Conversion Charter School is an existing public school that has been given charter status. In other words, it is a public school that has been converted to a charter school. After the changeover, the school is governed by itself, the local board of education, and the State Board of Education. The charter is governed solely by the local and state board as a third party to the contract.

A Start-Up Charter School is one that has been established by private organizations, state entities, local entities or individuals. It is operated under the charter petition, its local board of education, and the State Board of Education, which is a third party to the contract.

A LEA Startup Charter School is created by the local educational agency in the respective state. This type of charter school operates under the terms of the charter. It is managed by the charter petitioner, the local board of education, and the State Board of Education.

A State Chartered Special School is a State Board of Education approved public school. A State Charter petition becomes approved if the local board denies the original charter that was submitted to the local board.

Charter schools continue to grow in popularity and several provisions have been made to facilitate the establishment of such schools. This is particularly so in the case of the conversion schools, where public schools are transformed into charter ones.

Charter School Structure and Programs

In the main, students are admitted to charter schools based on the application submission and enrollment phases and or guidelines. In the event that the school receives more applications than space available, the person's name goes into a lottery phase.

All students are entitled to an equal chance of being selected to a charter school; therefore, the school has no admittance policies.

Evidently, the popularity of chartered schools has grown at exponential rates because of the low performances of traditional public schools and other concerns that parents have with traditional public schools. Consequently, chances are that admissions to these schools may be done carelessly. Therefore, if students, parents and, in turn, society are to benefit from the school choice program, admissions have to be governed.

Unlike what many thought at the beginning of the charter school movement, charter schools did not create an elitist system. Rather, most of the enrollment and admissions of charter school students consist of children who are minorities. This has been statistically supported by Federal figures, which reveal that the enrollment of charter schools across the country reflect a higher percentage of minority students than those in the public school sector.

Funding Allotment

As successful as charter schools have been and as beneficial as they are to families with low-income, they have limited access to funding across America (local and state funding). Because most charter schools are non-profit organizations, the majority of the funds received is to secure, furnish, and maintain the facilities. Inevitably, this creates financial challenges for charter schools.

The reality is that many state laws do not provide full funding to public charter schools. As a matter of fact, the money they receive can be significantly lower than the norm. Others restrict the ability of the charter school to function to their maximum capacity by:

- Making funds unpredictable
- Delaying payments to schools
- Leaving it to the discretion of districts to determine how much they will pay their competitor charter schools
- Preventing local tax revenues from flowing to charter schools
- Making charter schools dependent on specific appropriations by legislators each year

In a separate study conducted by the Legislative Office of Educational Oversight in Ohio, it was found that the per-pupil operating funding was actually 9% less than that for district public school. However, since 16% of the money received by charters is spent on the facilities, they have much less than the district public schools to spend on instruction. This occurs although the local school district and State Board of Education are required by law to treat charter schools just as favorably as they do other local schools with the provision of funding for basic services.

The charter school is expected to receive federal funds for special education programs based on the eligibility of the students that it serves. All other funds are expected to come from independent sources. Obviously, there has been much discussion about the intent of some to sabotage the charter movement. Therefore, more research needs to be done to assess the impact the lack of funding has on the long-term stability of charter schools across America.

Politics of Chartering

Authorizers have the legal right to issue charters, but this differs from state to state just as bodies that are legally entitled to operate under such charters. Usually, the state board of education authorizes charters; however, in other states, local school districts may be authorized to issue charters. Charter-initiated bodies whose intention it is to operate charter schools may include local school districts, initiations of higher education, non-profit corporations, and for-profit corporations. For-profit corporations are mainly authorized to operate charter schools in Michigan and California. There is the contention that for-profit charter schools are using the funds to maintain profits. Plus, some believe that for-profit charter schools seldom outperform traditional schools even when they receive higher funding.

The state dictates the funding of these schools. Charter school funding is dictated by the state with funds being transferred from the district in which the student lives. The Federal Elementary and Secondary Education Act also authorizes funding grants for charter schools. Private donors of foundations can also provide money to run these schools.

Minnesota became the first state to adopt the charter school law and started the first charter school in 1991. California quickly followed suit in 1992. This was the start of the increase in charter schools across the U.S. as 19 other states passed charter laws to implement change in public education. By the year 2016, over 45 states had started charter schools, including Puerto Rico and the District of Columbia.

There is no doubt that the number of charter schools across America has grown exponentially over the years. Actually, the charter school is perhaps, one of the fastest growing innovations in education policy. It has gained strong bipartisan support from governors, state legislators and past and present Secretaries of Education and with the support of former and current Presidents.

In 1997 in his State of the Union address, former President

Bill Clinton called for the creation of 3,000 charter schools by the year 2002. In 2002, President Bush called for $2000 million to support charter schools. He also budgeted for another $100 million for a new Credit Enhancement for the Charter Schools Facilities Program. The U.S Department of Education also approved grants to support the states' charter school efforts. This started with a $6 million-dollar allotment in the fiscal year 1995.

During the last year of President George W. Bush's administration, the budget for charter schools was $208 million. In 2016, it was $333.2 million with President Obama. An Obama-Biden administration provided the expanded charter school funding only to states that improve accountability for charter schools, allowing for interventions in struggling charter schools and providing a clear process for closing down chronically underperforming charter schools.

An Obama-Biden administration also prioritized supporting states that help the most successful charter schools to expand to serve more students.

Under President Trump, DeVos's Education Department planned to spend an unprecedented amount of public money — well over $1 billion — to expand school choice in the 2018 proposed budget and has considered other ways to promote choice. The Secretary has not been shy about expressing disdain for the traditional public school system by calling it a "dead end" and a "monopoly."

Parental Satisfaction

Parental satisfaction is essential to the success of the charter school. Thus, parents' knowledge of the school and their contribution to it are very important. They should also understand the advantages and attributes of the school.

In most cases, parents tend to learn about the charter schools from friends and relatives, which is quite similar to how parents learn about the traditional schools. However, several parents indicated they had never heard about the charter schools and their open enrollment even after several of the schools were in operation for over 5 years.

Over a five-year study period, parents indicated they enrolled their children in charter schools mainly because of the high test scores, the teaching of moral values, and because of better discipline. In the traditional schools, parents were more concerned about safety and teaching moral values. Safety was never ranked as one of the major concerns in charter schools.

> Over a five-year study period, parents indicated they enrolled their children in charter schools mainly because of the high test scores, the teaching of moral values, and because of better discipline.

Obviously, based on various data and surveys, the majority of parents were not at all happy with the school their children attended before the charter school. Their satisfaction levels were much higher with the charter schools than the traditional public schools.

Without charter schools, it seems like most parents would send their children to neighborhood schools, and the others would be at private religious schools, magnet public schools; some would have been homeschooled, or sent to private non-religious school. Inevitably, some would have dropped out of school.

Effective School Characteristics

According to Lawrence Lezotte, what constitutes a school as being effective is dependent upon the characteristics of the school correlated to its goals. He conducted a study that showed a correlation of effective schools and effective qualities and/or characteristics, originally created by the late Ronald Edmond. Moreover, the research for effective characteristics is credited to Ronald Edmonds, who implemented a unique study with several schools in California, analyzing what was effective and what was not.

Conclusions have been made over time, some controversial, on how effective public schools are and what constitutes an effective school. Some research suggested that public schools did not make a significant difference in the educational system. The Equality of Educational Opportunity Report gave credit to the family backgrounds of students as the main reason they were successful in school. He proposed that those children from poor families and homes that lacked good conditions and values that were necessary to support education, could not learn regardless of what the school did.

When successful schools were compared with similar schools, in like neighborhoods, where children were not learning, or learning at a low level, the basic conclusion was:

- Public schools do make a difference, including the ones that have students from poor backgrounds.
- Children from poor backgrounds have the ability to learn at high levels as a result of public schools.
- There are unique characteristics and processes common to schools where all children are learning, regardless of family background

The studies also revealed there are certain characteristics of schools that determine how effective they are, such as:

SCHOOL CHOICE CHARACTERISTICS

1. An orderly environment/safe environment
2. Involvement of parents/parental involvement
3. Respect for diversity in cultures and environments
4. High cohesion and collaboration
5. Principals providing abundant support for their teachers/ professional development
6. Engaged active learning and academic success/time on task

Along with the above, there are several other characteristics that are associated with the quality of a school. These characteristics enhance a community of learners and promote achievement.

Clearly, many families are happy with the school reform movement. They are grateful for the opportunity to have school choice, because they want to send their children to schools that are effective. Charter schools have been successful in attaining the characteristics of effective schools and so, parents are opting to send their children to charter schools.

"Give me six hours to chop down a tree and I will spend the first four sharpening the axe."

~ Abraham Lincoln

HISTORY OF DATE

CHARTERING SUCCESS

My tenure as the Chief Executive Officer (CEO) of the DeKalb Academy of Technology and Environment (DATE) suffered an acrimonious beginning. I entered a professional atmosphere riddled with turmoil and infighting between DATE's Board of Directors (the Board) and its former leadership. I was vying for the position of DATE's principal at the time, so I subjected myself to several interviews with the former CEO and the Board of Directors (as it was then constituted) at their behest. DATE's former leadership informed me that the Board no longer wanted to consider me under their employ; an announcement contradicted by the Board subsequent request that I subject myself to their interview process yet again. After a series of bewildering and surreal setbacks, I was finally afforded the position of not only Principal, but DATE's CEO months later, after my interview by the Board in the year 2006.

My first impression of DATE was remarkable. DATE's students were proud, enthusiastic, brilliant and respectful members of the charter school, formerly known as 'LATE.' LATE was an acronym, which stood for the Lithonia Academy of Technology and the Environment; a charter school, whose attendees were primarily residents of Lithonia City. There was a transition between LATE and DATE occurring at the time when I joined LATE, which was in May, just before summer began. My responsibility during this time was to assist with the changeover and to make general observations. What a shocking revelation it was, to discover that of the two hundred students enrolled in LATE, more than half would be forcibly dismissed by the end of the academic year; a desperate and spiteful act of retaliation from dissatisfied parents over the exodus of the former leadership. In addition, more than 2 dozen teachers would have to be interviewed and hired in under a months' time – all under my new leadership.

HISTORY OF DATE

This revenge tactic understandably angered the children's parents; or at least, it was what I deemed the root of their frustration. One day, nearly 180 parents congregated on the school's compounds to complain about LATE's Board and its departing leadership. I politely honored their requests to withdraw their children from LATE. By the end of May, this mass exodus reduced LATE's enrolment to about 40 students. The students' parents, despite our accidence to their requests, had grievances with LATE's Board. I was not a favorite among them.

It was next at this time that I was to be formally introduced and the board would vote to hire me as the new Headmaster/CEO that would take place at the official Board of Director's Meeting. My introduction to the parents of the students still enrolled in LATE was more like an interrogation of and a retaliation against its Board during my placement as their CEO. The school was initially operated out of a church, and I was presented in the sanctuary behind the pulpit. At least I had God's Protection!

I was cognizant of the different challenges which lay before me. I prepared a presentation, which meticulously explained the school's new vision, mission and core values. It also took considerable time and effort to conceptualize and outline a cohesive plan of action designed to shift the school's reputation from ordinary to outstanding, which I used to demonstrate to the remaining and concerned parents that I meant business. This was not the first time I was tasked with revamping a school's general academic performance from the ground up; I oversaw and was chiefly responsible in bringing about a similar transformation with another school as its principal and administrator, who worked closely with the school's superintendent to close the achievement gap using effective, impactful and student-driven initiatives.

CHARTERING SUCCESS

My preparation emboldened me to address the most difficult questions and comments that I could reasonably anticipate. My presentation's end was not met by shouts and boos of disapproval, but they were drowned out by the overwhelming cheers and joviality of a standing ovation. Some of the questions, which followed led to discussions about overhauling the students' curriculum. Other questions raised concerns about testing and other means of assessing the students' scholastic aptitude. None of the questions posed to me roused feelings of hesitation or doubt, and I answered them all with confidence. After I elaborated on how I intended to carry LATE upwards and onwards towards greatness, I was escorted outside the building and encountered a peaceful protest, which several news agencies reported the objection to my new assignment.

Despite the contentious atmosphere and the fact that the protest was organized against my appointment, I was able and willing to answer any questions the protestors had. I presented a cordial and understanding attitude as I addressed each of the parents' queries. I also learned that the parents were disgusted not by my appointment, but by the former leadership's ousting from her position. Apparently, this individual was trusted and revered by the students' parents for their direct involvement in LATE's founding. Once I answered the protestor's questions, they eventually dispersed. All the Board's members were quick to throw their support behind me after that.

> My preparation emboldened me to address the most difficult questions and comments that I could reasonably anticipate.

The next order of business was to replace the 200+ students, who left LATE prior to the end of the academic year.

HISTORY OF DATE

One day, while I was busy attempting to solve this problem, I encountered a lady, who had the most beautiful smile and outgoing personality I had ever seen. She was a former member of the Board, and a parent, whose children were enrolled in LATE. Her charisma and engagement in outreach convinced me that she would be the ideal student recruiter. With the end of May fast approaching, I had less than a month to matriculate at least 200 children into LATE, employ staff to educate them, and furnish the staff with the appropriate resources.

LATE was registering children from all over DeKalb County as its students within the two months which followed. While I was, of course, grateful for this development, I also wondered, who or what was to thank for it. My curiosity got the better of me one day, so I asked my newly hired recruiter, *"Where did you find all these students?"* She replied that she scouted barbershops, grocery stores, malls, residence and any other suitable location she was directed by God to search. When I heard this response, I felt comforted and assured that LATE, even in the face of its numerous hindrances, would prevail.

Speaking of hindrances, we discovered that LATE as an institution, owed back taxes and worker's compensation in the amount of $400,000.00. To make matters worse, LATE was being asked to relocate its premises. These were all obstacles, which suddenly appeared to impede LATE's progression to excellence. I knew within myself that my conquering of these obstacles was part of God's Divine Plan for me and that it would have been impossible for me to do so without having trust and faith in Him. With that in mind, my newly constituted Board and I began researching new locations and carefully considered how we would repay the $400,000.00.

CHARTERING SUCCESS

While brainstorming the ultimate solution to LATE's woes, I created a memorable and brand new name for the school. LATE's restructuring process was signified by the renaming of LATE to the aforementioned DATE (DATE includes the entire DeKalb County). In addition, DATE's Board and I decided that exclusivity would be in DATE's best interests. I proposed that our students wear uniforms consisting of green blazers and ties daily. Wearing uniforms establishes a routine, promotes decorum and creates distinction from other schools. How one dresses is how one will act, and presenting oneself in a manner, which exudes success, attracts success.

> Wearing uniforms establishes routine, promotes decorum and creates distinction from other schools.

Changing LATE's name was a good (but insufficient) step in the right direction. Another image, which was a direct reflection of the students' perception would also require an amendment: it was time to change the school's mascot! LATE's mascot was a turtle. Now, I have no issue with turtles, but they are inherently slow, and I did not want that slowness juxtaposed to my students' cognitive abilities. I wanted the mascot to represent DATE's students and its new mission and objectives, both of which were centered on technology and the environment. I recommended 'The Explorers' as our new mascot; an illustration, which is easily connected to DATE's goals.

With needing much financial resources, DATE was put in a compromising position, due to the mismanagement of funds by the former leadership; therefore, DATE had limited or no resources and creditworthiness with vendors. For this reason, I became the vehicle in purchasing the curriculum, books, and

HISTORY OF DATE

programs with personal credit and savings. Of course, the academy certainly made allowances, but it would take a few years to reestablish trust and credit with creditors. It would all be worth it and I would do it all over again for the sake of teaching and learning that would be available for the academy kids.

In having to relocate in less than 20 days and a month before school, the time came for DATE to move into a new church facility with additional classrooms, state-of-the-art security alarm systems, and six trailers, which we moved to the new location. A disaster of sorts would impact DATE on its grand opening day of school, however: we learned the compound did not pass its fire inspection test. Upon receiving this unfortunate news, I met with DATE's Board of Directors as a matter of urgency and suggested, *"Since we were in the process of rebranding anyway, why do we need to remain in a building to educate our students? We can simply be explorers, just like our mascot."* This was our exact course of action. We rented 10 charter buses and traveled to various attractions which were relevant to the school's aims: museums, Stone Mountain Park, the Atlanta Zoo, the Botanical Gardens, the Fernbank Science Center, etc. We were dismayed to later discover that the trailers did not pass the fire inspection test, either! This meant that the classes for grades 5 – 8 would have to be held in the compound's gym.

We were reliably informed that the wooden deck, which surrounded the trailers was improperly constructed and needed to be rebuilt to comply with the fire code; a project which would be finished in one month and cost more than $100,000.00. In the meantime, we had 120 students housed in a gym within proximity to one another. This created not only its own host of problems, but also presented opportunities for the students and teachers to interact and motivate each other while they all adjusted. The students' families understood that though the atmosphere was somewhat uncomfortable, DATE's quality of education remained a priority.

We conducted classes in the school's gym for months. There were over 100 students, who spent the entire school day being taught one lesson after another. The trailers were subjected to another fire inspection, which they finally passed. This meant that all the trailers were now open for the students to use! Throughout my first year as CEO, DATE's challenges seem to dwindle as it makes its indelible mark on the surrounding communities. Swaths of parents and other community members volunteered to work with DATE. In fact, DATE's waiting list grew to well over 400 students, and the school received an outpouring of donated resources from community members and the local school district. DATE's process of reeducating students and molding them into productive members of society, together with its unique focus on activities and projects related to technology and the environment, ensured that DATE developed a stellar reputation for the foreseeable future. DATE also made house calls to not only teach students but their families.

> ... with its unique focus on activities and projects related to technology and the environment, ensured that DATE developed a stellar reputation for the foreseeable future.

Following several meetings with DATE's Board of Directors and many failed attempts to reach an agreement regarding the purchase of a few properties for DATE's benefit, I managed to convey to the Board to lease 50,000 square feet for office space. The building, which stood on the office space used to be the headquarters for a major advertisement trade company.

HISTORY OF DATE

I finalized the arrangements and we were able to relocate our base of operation to this space, though our budget was limited. To be honest, entering and making payments under the lease depleted a significant portion of DATE funds, which left the Board and me with limited revenue to hire an architecture firm to draft plans for the construction of over 30 classrooms and office space on the leased lot. With questions and optimism, DATE now had the resources to renovate the prospective building with having close to 3 quarters of a million dollars from the careful programming, planning, and strategic designing of savings for three years and savings of the school's for-profit, Aftercare Program – the dream was now becoming a reality.

DATE's progression to its fourth year of operation from its third was an exciting and rewarding experience for us all. DATE passed other vital inspections as the third academic year ended. We were well on our way to opening our new building to the public, but as fate would have it, yet another obstacle was placed before us: three days before the new academic year was scheduled to commence, DATE was denied a Certificate of Occupancy amid the enrolment of nearly 400 students. Would this be a repeat of DATE's first academic year? The students and teachers anxiously awaited the news. The decisive phone call came in; we were approved for a Certificate of Occupancy after all! Our approval was based on a grandfather clause.

Three years later, we were able to purchase DATE's building outright and renovate. I recall attending a convention, where I encountered an architect I worked with regarding another school district. I was introduced to an individual who sold municipal bonds. With municipal bonds, one only required: approval for a specific amount of money; and to have the said amount agreed upon by the local municipality. Once these simple steps were taken, the money would be disbursed to us... or so we thought. The process has a plethora of checks and balances related to DATE's financial status and its good standing as an academic institution, both of which needed to be maintained at a level well above average.

Following lengthy discussions and meetings with attorneys and representatives of three different municipalities, DATE was awarded a $7,500.000.00 municipal bond to purchase the new facility, a new gym and cafeteria, with contemporary classrooms to meet the students' needs. This day ushered in a new spirit of excellence, passion and a determination to succeed. Additionally, our savings enabled DATE to receive a BBB+ rating from Standard & Poor's Financial Services LLC, an American financial services company and global rating agency. 'BBB+' was one of the highest credit ratings a K-8 school had earned.

When DATE opened its doors to the public, it introduced exceptional staff, extraordinary students and superb parents into their fold. Since then, DATE maintains a waiting list of over 500 students annually. The academic scores achieved by DATE's students are over and above the local and state's testing average. DATE continues to be a premier charter school, which teaches its students to be competitive and confident leaders in the fields of technology and science! As DATE had begun to emerge as a schoolhouse full of initiatives, hopes, and expectations in educating her brightest, she soon developed into a beacon of success, where the community, parents, students, and teachers all shared and basked in the celebration of quality education that rivals no other. Her teachings in freedom of expression and uniqueness provide all with enrichment and wholeness for all that seek that ultimate and engaging learning experience.

"Without change there is no innovation, creativity, or incentive for improvement. Those who initiate change will have a better opportunity to manage the change that is inevitable."

~ William Pollard

What Really Matters in a Charter School: Our Successes and Framework

The mission of the DATE charter school under study included the goals of a technological and environmental emphasis. In keeping with such an emphasis, the school aims to educate the student population on the vital question of the environmental ramifications of technology and other business decisions via a hands-on, instructional curriculum. To this end, the school's objective is to enhance student achievement by using a curriculum that:

- Recognizes the important link between technology and the environment.

- Promotes higher order thinking, critical thinking, problem-solving, and decision-making skills.

- Motivates students by offering a real-world context for learning.

- Engages learners in investigative, hands-on/minds-on, student-centered, and cooperative activities between the industry and environmental groups.

- Advances educational reform goals.

- Meets state and national academic standards.

- Considers the environment in its totality with the co-existence of business and the natural surroundings.

- Promotes continuous lifelong learning.

But, the objectives of the charter school do not end there. The wider goal of the charter school also includes providing a conceptual framework for the learning processes within an effective school. That is to say, the charter school also advocates the imaginative use of the curriculum to encourage in-depth, hands-on studies of the students' life within the community. By this means, it aims to accomplish the following six goals:

- Enhance the students' enthusiasm about learning for better academic performance.

- Increase the enthusiasm of teachers towards learning and teaching so they would be more innovative in the classroom.

- Motivate students to be more involved in their communities, both as students and in adult life. When the students are exposed to the complexity of real-world issues, they will become more enlightened when dealing with socio-economic developments around them. They will also gain an appreciation of how their communities and natural surroundings relate to one another.

- Enhance student understanding of the real-world consequences of political decisions, thereby increasing their interest and participation in the political process.

- Teach students to act responsibly and consider the environmental implications of business decisions.

Such a conceptual framework assumes primarily that goals frame actions, thoughts, and feelings. This perspective is considered the dominant one when studying achievement, especially educational achievement. When dealing with the complex set of processes and specific outcomes as goals, the aim is to show a cluster of competencies that can be measured.

Research studies have further suggested that the characteristics of school satisfaction depend on a large sample population and the assessment of school inputs and outcomes.

Such studies have tended to place more emphasis on measuring the resources of schools rather than the manner in which those resources were organized and used.

However, in 1981, Richard Murnane proposed that the resources of a school, or "school matters," played a major role in school achievement. The primary resources of teachers and students, as well as, the secondary resources: the physical facilities, class size, curriculum, and instructional strategies are all factors that affect student learning through their collective influence on the behavior of teachers and students alike. These relationships among parents, teachers, and students would have a strong bearing on the curriculum and instructional methods, parent participation, professional development, shared governance, and engagement. Such inputs would determine the level of satisfaction that stakeholders perceive in the charter school in terms of real outcomes such as political participation, achievement, motivation, and enthusiasm as well as an appreciation for the environment. There is no doubt that the curriculum and instruction, professional development, shared governance and the engagement of both students and parents are all essential for the success and satisfaction of its students. To this end, school reform efforts in technology and the environment will have to go beyond textbook learning and look into teaching methods and the wider applications the school has established.

> ...school reform efforts in technology and the environment will have to go beyond textbook learning...

WHAT REALLY MATTERS IN A CHARTER SCHOOL

Curriculum and Instruction

Environmental issues will play a dominant role among the specific objectives set out in the charter school's curriculum. The environment is inherently far more captivating for children than coursework in the traditional curriculum, all the more when children are encouraged to observe and learn from the dynamics of their environment. Such exposure will have a more meaningful and lasting impression on them. Thus, the learning environment is shifting beyond the four walls of the classroom to outdoor natural settings. The reformed school encourages the class to move into places where there are trees, in the playground and other open places where the children can learn through exposure.

Environmental influence can be mixed and not always positive. In the county, where one charter school attempted to apply the outdoor method of learning, it was found that the geology of the area had led to its progress from aboriginal trading villages to the quarries that epitomize it today. Such economic developments had, on the one hand, positive effects and on the other, negative in terms of the environment, history, the economy, and even the demographics.

The lesson to be learned is that, unless environmental issues are assessed, understood, and managed in the right way, the very thing that caused the county's progress could pose a threat. This locale truly presents an opportunity for the charter school's stakeholders to understand the complexities of life's continuum through a very real-life case study.

Shared Governance

Studies show that shared governance is directly related to teacher performance and teaching methods that are practiced and proven to be effective. With innovative teaching, the charter school can reap the benefits of increased school satisfaction and performance in and outside the classroom.

A school that has a strong and shared leadership involving all of the stakeholders will achieve its goal of reform as seen in high-performance, low dropout rates, and satisfaction. According to the current research, there is no denying the importance of the link between leadership and student achievement. This is particularly true when the leadership takes the initiative to shape teaching and learning. When members of a school community are empowered to make decisions, a more collaborative effort is achieved. As staff, administrators, parents, community members, and students become an important part of the team, much more can be accomplished, and the "we" factor kicks in.

This shared governance approach enables sound decisions to be made by those closest to the students in the charter school, because of its autonomy and higher levels of trust among stakeholders. Staff can share leadership responsibilities and autonomy with principals in the areas of staffing, budget, curriculum and assessment, governance, and scheduling. This allows each community to structure itself according to the students' needs. Staff get to have inputs in the decisions that will affect the school, the students, and themselves. Since they are included in the decision-making, they have a greater sense of responsibility and pride in what they do.

> A school that has a strong and shared leadership involving all of the stakeholders will achieve its goal of reform...

Professional Development

It goes without saying that professional learning and development is a prerequisite to stability and progress in educational reform. That is why in the reform charter school, professional development should be the norm, not the exception.

In this way, effective techniques derived from professional development can be used to the fullest in the classroom. Lesson plans are required and, depending on the topic, may cover several weeks at a stretch. The school principal monitors the preparation of these lesson plans, which are submitted to the local board upon request. As the children mature, the teachers take on the role of learning facilitators as they are not the only source of knowledge. The students, at their young age, are already encouraged to learn from their peers, from reference resources (including computer and media center), and from actively participating in measurement, record-keeping and drawing conclusions regarding project-oriented tasks.

Furthermore, practical training at least once a month, gives the staff exposure to best practices. Great emphasis is also placed on teachers exploring and developing new lesson plans by using environmental and technological resources advocated by the curriculum.

Financially, teachers, who have relevant environmental, technological and related know-how should be considered to be assets and thus rewarded on the basis of their specialized as well as interactive training. The following are the requirements for teachers in the charter school:

- All teachers are required to engage in pre-service training by the use of programs and projects about the history and philosophy of this curriculum.
- They have also been taught how to source resources relevant to the curriculum, including books and

internet-based material, and to adopt innovative ways of teaching this skill.

- Teachers must have Gifted Certification Endorsement to enhance, identify, and nurture the varied and unique learning styles of their students.

- Teachers should have in-service training on an ongoing basis each school year.

- A minimum of 10 hours of such training should be set aside for an environmentally and technologically attuned curriculum. Additionally, the reform entails availability for faculty use of publications entitled "Environmental Education Materials." All training sources must comply with this goal.

- Teachers should aim to become Google Classroom Certified Teachers to enhance technology integration.

- Teachers will have been exposed to STEAM training and have completed Art class certification in partnership with Georgia Piedmont Technical College.

Documentation of all training will also be forwarded to the Local Board quarterly. Teachers who do not satisfy these requirements without reasonable explanation will not be rehired. A good benchmark for the faculty's appreciation of and commitment to the curriculum should be its low teacher turnover rate, showing teacher satisfaction.

Parental Participation

Both parental involvement and school partnership in the success and satisfaction of a school is a potent combination.

WHAT REALLY MATTERS IN A CHARTER SCHOOL

Schools that encourage active PTA/PTO involvement in their activities and decision making, inevitably reap the best rewards.

The charter school reform that has been established also encourages parental initiative in petitions, school governance, finances, organizational structure, and student activities. In this way, parents, members of the community, and other interested parties will be actively involved in school affairs.

Due to concerns about certain public schools in the local district, a group of parents took the initiative to investigate viable alternatives. They discovered the Arabia Mountain Heritage Area Alliance. For years, this alliance had contemplated establishing a local charter school that could take advantage of the unique educational opportunities presented by an Arabia Mountain environmental group. The two parties then collaborated and explored the possibility of establishing a reform model school. The Alliance did an excellent job of supporting the parents, providing them with considerable information and resource banks related to the type of school and reforms they wanted.

The upshot is that parents, members of the community, and other interested parties are now involved in the school in many different ways:

- Active participation in the school: serving on its board, volunteering in and out of the classroom, membership in a Parent Teacher Organization (PTO), and serving on various committees set up by its Board;

- Involvement in the day-to-day role of supervising the progress of their children by participating in a mandatory 20 hours a month. This includes helping their children with at-home projects, attending school performances and events, and transporting them to and from school;

- Assistance in the school performance assessment process by participating in survey polls.

Community involvement is very extensive. Community representatives sit on the school board, one from the community sector, educational sector, and one from the technology sector. Without a doubt, the implementation of the school reform charter and the curriculum's focus on specialization, have achieved satisfaction in terms of the school's and the students' success. Such achievement has been demonstrated by the students' ability to master higher order thinking skills, namely:

> ...the school scored high marks in parental and community participation, which in no small way contributed to the success of the charter school.

- Critical thinking
- Problem-solving
- Decision-making
- Motivation to learn with a continuum of knowledge
- Recognition of conflict
- Recognition of the need to reconcile competing societal interests

In addition, the school scored high marks in parental and community participation, which, in no small way, contributed to the success of the charter school.

The framework for this study covered the resourced characteristics of the charter school, specifically that concerning the curriculum, parental and student involvement, as well as professional development and engagement.

The effective characteristics of the school included a study of various points of view: integration of school satisfaction and the search for additional insights in other theoretical traditions, such as organizational, curricular and behavioral theories, organizational learning, and human resource management. These theories clearly identified the characteristics or factors that are essential for increased levels of satisfaction in the students, in the learning and teaching process, and in the educational setting.

Summary

The purpose of the study was to determine if the satisfaction levels of the charter school could be used as the benchmark for student achievement and success. The research was based on the examination of school-related documents, as well as, participant interviews to capture their varied experiences and perceptions. This would help us arrive at a fuller understanding of the way to examine and apply the concept of satisfaction.

A theoretical framework propounded by Schemes and Demesue in 2005 was used in this research process to make predictions and to provide explanations relating to the essential perceptions of what constitute effective school goals. Such a framework could explain and predict the factors that would assist the practitioner to better understand the variables underpinning and contributing to the mechanisms of empirical work.

"In every problem, there's a concealed solution, locking itself underneath, unlock, peruse, find and solve."

~ Michael Bassey Johnson

WHAT THE DATA REVEALS ABOUT A SUCCESSFUL CHARTER SCHOOL

The purpose of the case study was to examine how satisfied teachers, parents, and students were with the DATE charter school based on its goals and objectives, that is:

- Enhancing teacher enthusiasm about learning and teaching to bring more innovative instructional strategies into the classroom

- Encouraging students to become more involved in their communities, making students gain an appreciation for how their community and natural surroundings relate to one another.

- Enhancing student understanding of the real-world consequences of political decisions,

- Teaching students to act responsibly and consider environmental/technological implications that will be based on the perceptions of stakeholders of parents, students, and teachers.

Several questions were addressed in this study, which required multiple approaches to collect and verify information and capture the various perceptions that exist. An analysis of the data will also be presented over a one-year period with a view to evaluating the factors that determine charter school satisfaction: parental participation, curriculum and instruction, engagement and shared governance.

This study was done on students in grades 1 - 8, who were enrolled in the charter school, the parents of students, who were enrolled in those specified grades of the charter school, and the teachers and classified staff members employed by the charter school in those specified grades.

On completion of the surveys, focus groups, and

WHAT THE DATA REVEALS

interviews in this case study, the stakeholders will be aware of some of the significant contributing goals of a charter school that leads it to the point where it can achieve stakeholder satisfaction in performance and academic achievement. In this case, the researcher captured relevant information discovered from examining the goals the charter school wanted to accomplish and in what ways those goals led to performance, satisfaction, and reform in this context.

> Charter schools focus mainly on reforming and improving the way teaching and learning are done in schools.

We explored the environment of the charter school in an attempt to identify the specific influences that are effective in producing satisfaction in the performance of charter schools.

In addition, we took a look at the satisfaction level in the accomplishment of school goals by using the methods of:

- Individual interviews
- Observations
- School demographic documents.

The interviews were transcribed and scripted. From this, themes were identified. In conjunction with an analysis of relative documents, findings were made and conclusions were reached. To fully understand the charter school implications, it is important to consider the individual's own perceptions and subjective apprehensions.

What perceptions of satisfaction produce the desired outcomes of achievement in a charter school? Charter schools focus mainly on reforming and improving the way teaching and learning are done in schools. They pay close attention, not only to students learning, but the participation and involvement of stakeholders in achieving the school's mission, as it may differ from other schools' focus. This study depicts such differences. Various methods were used to collect qualitative data to supplement, validate, explain, illuminate, and reinterpret the quantitative data.

The perceptions people have of a known activity are valuable to the field of education, because it is important for stakeholders to know the components and elements of curriculum and instruction, parental participation, professional development, engagement, and shared governance. It is equally important for them to know, whether or not, these same components have improved the overall school and student achievement.

The data was collected with the intention to provide feedback and valuable information to the charter school to assist them in making improvements. It also helps to address the goals of the charter school reform movement generally.

Interview Question Categories

The research study provided teachers, parents, students and the public with an overview of these processes. Parents, students, teachers, administrators, and community members all participated in the research interviews and answered questions about the topics below. The interviews were conducted at the local charter school site and after compiling data, common themes started to emerge. Interview questions were asked in the following areas:

- Learning engagement
- Clubs and activities

WHAT THE DATA REVEALS

- Neighborhood care
- Environmental importance
- Clean, orderly and environmentally safe communities
- Participation in decision-making at the school
- Shared governance

Interview Response Summary

The interview transcripts disclosed that the study participants believed that student/teacher engagement was evident and considered the norm for favorable teaching practices for the charter school's students. The study participants praised the charter school for its innovative and unique strategies geared towards augmenting student learning and engagement during the study's tenure. The study has made it clear that teachers are granted the opportunity and freedom to explore creative ways of transforming the standard processes of teaching and learning in a meaningful and impactful way.

The responses to the interview questions made by teachers, parents, and students revealed that learning includes the charter school's students being present and active in the learning centers alongside their teachers. The responses to the interview questions further reveal that the use of technology and project-based learning increases both student and teacher engagement.

The interview transcripts also disclosed that the words 'recycling' and 'environment' recurred consistently throughout the study. Participants stated that the Beta Club, Boy Scouts, Girl Scouts, Environmental Club, STEAM Club, and Technology Club, were unparalleled in the success of the recycling and conservation initiatives.

'Going green' is trending in the charter school due to the positive influence of the clubs and organizations over those teachers, parents, and students, who are legitimately concerned about safeguarding the environment. The students, who are not members of the Beta Club, nevertheless, praised its service to the charter school and the wider community. The other organizations such as Basketball, Track and Field, Spanish Club, and Cheerleading were all mentioned throughout the study, but it became clear that certain clubs and organizations were more popular than others, and as such, were the most active, according to several of the participants selected for interviews. What also became clear is that a significant percentage of students participate in extracurricular activities associated with the charter school.

The clubs and organizations primarily raise funds and provide assorted services for the members of the charter school's community and local neighborhood. Their formation started with parents volunteering to spearhead and sponsor activities for the students who attend the charter school. All but one local club or organization have a parent sponsor, who is responsible for their management.

> 'Going green' is trending in the charter school due to the positive influence of the clubs and organizations...

The interview transcripts disclosed that participants were keenly aware of the importance of recycling, protecting and taking care of the environment. The community the charter school is located in is replete with natural resources and strongly emphasizes recycling and conservation efforts. The charter school's founders and constituents proposed that teaching its students the significance of conservation and sustainability in the community would, in turn, embolden those students to advocate for the preservation of its environment.

There are also recycling days, conservation days, sustainability days, environmental days, technology days, all inclusive of our STEAM celebration. All of these environmental and technology initiatives are integrated into daily lessons on how to make learning relative, interesting, and rigorous. With the addition of poultry farming, aquaponics, the organic farming, digital animation, media production, and coming soon, electric cars and aviation, the charter school has taken on the initiative to challenge students and provide stakeholders with career readiness skills and aptitude application. Students are learning to become aware about sustainability and conservation, while enhancing their innovative and creative talents.

The interview transcripts disclosed that governance was shared among teachers, parents, and students. Such shared governance is made evident through the charter school's governance structure, parent/teacher organization ("PTO") participation, volunteerism, student clubs and organizations, allocated resources, school campaigns, and management structures. The charter school's founders and constituents have proposed that shared governance be a vital component of the charter school's composition.

Teachers assume leadership positions to make recommendations with regards to prospective employees, as part of the interview process for those seeking employment at the charter school. Moreover, the faculty and staff are responsible for researching and developing the charter school's curriculum. The staff development process is set up in such a way that the voices of both faculty and staff can be heard.

Parents play a critical role in the governance structure of the charter school. The governance board consists of 9 members (6 of whom are parents elected to serve on the board), who formulate and enforce school policy. These parents actively make decisions that affect the overall structure of the charter school and impact on its petition reliability. Parents fundraise for the charter school and provide additional financial resources for expenditures, which are neither allocated nor supported by the local school district.

In this regard, the PTO has been instrumental in raising more than $50,000 for resources, such as Interactive Technology Smart Boards and projectors for all the charter school's classrooms, outdoor classroom equipment, environmental and technology learning tools, and additional learning resources. To support the limited number of faculty and staff on hand, many parents volunteered to assist teachers in numerous, valuable ways. Parents also act as substitute teachers throughout the year when necessary.

The SGA and class representatives are included in decision-making processes with respect to the charter school's clubs, organizations, activities, and resources (if it is appropriate for them to be included). Students meet on a weekly and monthly basis to discuss celebratory events, field trips and any other substantial topic that impacts on the student body.

Other Success Factors

Additional questions were posed during the interview that contributed to the analysis of the realization of the charter school's objectives:

- Are students performing differently at charter schools compared with those in other schools?

WHAT THE DATA REVEALS

- What more can be done to enable students to understand the information being presented to them?

The responses from the study participants support the belief that the charter school students perform better academically, because the teachers teach in a manner that is not just theoretical, but practical. What the students learn is therefore relevant to them in their lives. Students have at their disposal many ways of understanding what they are taught, and they are equipped with the tools to share the processes by which they learn with others.

Some parents have stated that their children are doing better socially, because the charter school makes a concerted effort to prepare students to build interpersonal relationships. These parents have also stated that their children are more articulate, can more confidently express themselves, and that the tutelage they receive from the charter school's teachers is responsible for these positive developments.

> **Students have at their disposal many ways of understanding what they are taught.**

In addition, the charter school's teachers are fulfilling the objectives of each child's specific needs and are making a special effort to assist them wherever possible. The students indicated that they are learning a lot about technology, and about the changes in the environment. They reported that school is 'fun.'

Community members have indicated that they have observed personal, professional and academic growth in all the students of the charter school within the past year, and can, therefore, testify with the utmost confidence that the students and parents alike appreciate what the school is seeking to accomplish.

Emerging Themes

The themes which emerged from the findings and observations are expanded as follows:

- **'Student/teacher involvement'** refers to the strategies used to involve children and teachers in teaching and learning processes that are relevant to the real world. 'Teacher creativity' refers to the way each teacher teaches, questions students, focuses on how individual students assimilate information, and implements games suited for learning.
- **'Civil participation and values'** refer to various organizations, such as the Boy Scouts, Girl Scouts, Technology Club, Environmental Club, Beta Club, Environmental Club, STEAM Club, and Student Government Association ("SGA"), together with the opportunities they provide students to take part in civic and community activities that cultivate healthy morals and respect for civil liberties.
- **'Recycling, conservation, sustainability, and the protection of the environment'** refer to the efforts of the charter school body to be actively involved in its recycling, sustainability and conservation programs, which also extend to the homes and communities of the body's members. The program pays attention to the recycling of paper, plastic, glass, and metal. The environmental curriculum addresses life, the Earth and natural science as integrated into the Georgia Curriculum (which the charter school has accommodated by increasing the length of the school day by 45 minutes. This decision serves as further reinforcement of the charter school's objectives).

WHAT THE DATA REVEALS

- **'Shared governance'** refers to the involvement of teachers, parents, and students in activities such as fundraising, classroom support, and the pooling of financial resources. In addition, the charter school requires that all parents, with children enrolled in it, allocate at least 20 hours towards accommodating local political decision-making. Students play a vital role in general decision-making as well, with the Student Government Association and Class Representatives taking part in fielding student concerns, resolving school-related issues and participating in charter school activities. A third of the charter school's Governing Board comprises the parents of some of its students.

The stakeholders are satisfied that the charter school's objectives have been achieved. The widespread acceptance of the charter school's objectives has resulted in a buy-in from most students, teachers, and parents. This buy-in has pervaded the charter school's culture and promoted a nurturing and viable community of individuals, who are destined to attain greatness in their future.

In conclusion, the success of the students enrolled in the charter school is measured by their ability to master higher-order thinking skills, critical thinking, problem-solving, decision-making, continuous learning, and conflict resolution.

The charter school has experienced dramatic growth since its inception over the years. Generally, student enrollment and parental involvement have increased, and teacher/student relationships have strengthened. In addition, the school's commitment to fulfilling its objectives continues to be one of its strongest points. The charter school has thus proven to be fairly successful; its students' test scores are continually rising and surpassing those earned by the students of the local district and state in certain categories.

A majority of the parents of the charter school's students now volunteer and contribute in diverse ways to their children's education. Specific initiatives like recycling and conservation continue to engage the students and advance their involvement within the charter school and the community.

The uniqueness of the charter school lies in the level of autonomy and creativity that it fosters through the teaching and learning processes employed by its teachers.

With respect to the levels of satisfaction within charter schools, the various entities which make up the education system must unite to effect the changes that are necessary for that system. This charter school model can become the ideal model for sustaining schooling at all levels, which would help avoid the pitfall of lack of public education support.

*"Not every puzzle is intended to be solved.
Some are in place to test your limits.
Others are, in fact, not puzzles at all."*

~ Vera Nazarian

PUTTING THE PIECES TOGETHER

CHARTERING SUCCESS

After examination, DeKalb Academy of Technology and Environment (DATE) is seen to have created a distinct school environment. This is the result of an educational program based on contemporary research in purposeful, effective, instructional, and non-instructional variables, all of which contribute to conditions that develop an effective and successful charter school.

Pillars of Effective Schools

The puzzle pieces that were discussed and researched included: autonomy, accountability, responsibility, cutting through bureaucracy, non-isolation, and creativity. These are the pillars of effective schools that are instructionally sound and culturally responsive. It has been found that such schools improve and increase overall student development. It is evident that autonomy is critical for teachers and instructors to create engaging and unique opportunities conducive to learning.

Moving away from traditional teaching methods and irrelevant learning experiences have yielded better results. At the same time, customizing the learning experiences of each individual student ensures that high levels of interest and connection are sustained. The experience goes beyond having the desired levels of knowledge. It extends to a level of caring, confidence, and passion in the teaching and learning process! That passion for learning is often channeled through our creativity, which contributes to strong personality traits, such as risk-taking, a sense of adventure, and independence.

> Moving away from traditional teaching methods and irrelevant learning experiences have yielded better results.

PUTTING THE PIECES TOGETHER

Our creativity has the power to deepen the student's understanding of their relationship to the world.

You see, at some point in life, we also have to experience some level of disruption and risk-taking. We must reach beyond the normalcy of what is expected or desired. In doing so, we will acquire the self-confidence and creativity to overcome obstacles/challenges throughout our life.

Undesirable Puzzle Pieces

The perception of defeat can only be wiped away by the motivation to excel and succeed. Our teachers and staff have readily taken on the challenge to be different. They dare to be great and see themselves destined to be creative!

The motivation they have to create engaging and unique environments is comparable to none. Certainly, accountability and responsibility are the first steps in taking ownership of their different skills and talents. The academy is bent on reducing and even ending that undesirable puzzle piece of bureaucracy and politics. Clearly, bureaucracy limits potential. It stands in the way of forming truly positive human interactions and solid interpersonal relationships. We have made a stand against stunting any student's growth, or teacher's development. In pledging to discourage bureaucracy and politics, we uphold the yearnings of parents to be directly involved as decision-makers in their children's education.

The time is ripe and the technology is available for us to cut the paperwork, protocol, and business that prevent education from being the topmost priority in the system. In life, we need to understand all the obstacles that impede our progress. Then, we must find strategic alternative routes to urgently reach our goals. Similar to life, successful teaching and good school cultures don't come with formulas. However, they have a necessary condition: educators must feel free to act on their best instincts. Minute by minute, as they respond to students and one another, their focus must be on doing what's right.

As humans, we can only focus on one thing at a time, as sociologist Robert Merton observed. That's why it's vital for teachers to have the space to concentrate on how to best communicate the lesson to their students. Any diversion from that focus can lead to indifference, or boredom and will break the magic.

This is why we must bulldoze through school bureaucracy and politics. This is a giant diversion, focused on compliance to please others governing from afar. You can combat bureaucracy at any level by simply eliminating every minute you spend worrying about compliance that interferes with human interaction. This is the essence of effective teaching and learning.

Building Piece by Piece

As you look at the pieces of education – or even your life experiences – never be afraid to trust others or yourself. Dare to be uniquely different. You might just be 'wonderfully wrong.' And if you are, welcome the opportunity to break those pieces of your puzzle, change their direction and put them back in a new way. Doing that will let you realize you're *one step closer* to seeing the whole picture and having all the pieces connect at the precise points.

Build your life and your world just as you would a puzzle: piece by piece, step by step, section by section. At times, you may get frustrated or even bored. You may feel as though you'd rather give up. What should you do in such circumstances? *Know* that you have all the parts and pieces of life's puzzle, and the more

PUTTING THE PIECES TOGETHER

ways you try to place them where they belong, the more connections you discover. Soon, you will begin to visualize and discern images as they come together to form the overall vision of your life.

What does your puzzle look like? Do you have a vision? Are you forcing the pieces to fit where they don't belong? If it's the latter, take another look; revisit your approach, and keep trying. All the answers are on the inside of you. And at this very moment, a surprisingly stunning picture is revealing itself to you, one 'gift' at a time.

Ten Takeaways

Although stakeholders are a very influential part of the success in their schools, readers should also understand the value of participation, policy, and advocacy as a general citizen when it comes to the matters of better schooling and education. *Chartering Success* is dependent on everyone examining great instructional methods, philosophies, methodologies frameworks, support systems, and investing in the right human capital. Not only is this a proven method for success at the charter schools, but it can be duplicated at any level of learning institution that seeks to improve and enhance the quality and education.

1. **Effective Partnerships**

    Effective schools have viable and meaningful partnerships with parents, students, and the teaching community. To build a community of learners, educational entities must value the role of each stakeholder in the entire educational process of a child and realize the significant contributions of each entity. These contributions can be resources and tools, monetary donations, or shared and borrowed talents and skills.

Whichever the case, the community that learns and teaches together – succeeds!

2. Individual Motives

Students come to school for a variety of reasons: clubs, organizations, teachers, academics, socializing, etc. Therefore, we must connect with each child's motives and desires. Sometimes, the joy of coming to school in itself can be impelling enough.

> Hence, until we truly know otherwise, let's harness any and every ounce of non-academic ability we see.

Yes, their priorities may not always be the three R's. Rather, they may be the hidden talents, desires, or wants that are clamoring to be discovered. The child may have one unique musical or physical attribute waiting to be developed. It may be the one prized asset that gets noticed or affirmed for that child. Hence, until we truly know otherwise, let's harness any and every ounce of non-academic ability we see.

3. Learning with Relationships, Relevance, and Rigor

These are key components of a well-rounded education. We have found that many schools that successfully engage students in learning have several things in common:

   a. They set high academic standards and provide rigorous, meaningful instruction and support that all students can meet.

b. Their structure makes it possible to give students individual attention.

c. The teachers take an interest in the students' lives, drawing on their real-world experiences and current understandings to build new knowledge.

d. The teachers also show students the connections between success in school and long-term career plans.

e. Infusing students with the above three R's is the cornerstone of success, high levels of self-awareness, and global learning.

4. **Flexibility in the Learning Process**

Charter schools give students options on how and what they can learn. They also give parents the opportunity to get involved, showing them how and what they can do. Charter schools are viable alternatives to the traditional schools and, as such, give parents and students choices and control over the educational process.

Charter schools have more flexible curricula, budgets, and staffing. They have a greater ability to make quick and effective changes to meet a student's needs and provide a high level of accountability with review and renewal every five years.

They empower teachers to make important decisions that are beneficial to the students. And, finally, the parents are encouraged by the school to work alongside the teachers as a team to advance their children's academic progress.

5. Defining True School Success

Many variables define school success. The academic variable is just one facet of measurement. It does not determine the attainment of total success. In life, we measure the things we truly value. Therefore, this statement should be true about our schools. However, too often, it is not. Consider the things we measure: state test scores, perfect attendance, grades, office referrals – the list goes on. It isn't that these things aren't important; it's that they probably aren't the *most* important. All too often, the things we value and measure in our school system are not the ones that end up equating to student success later in life.

> Adults must provide educational influences to great life-long learning opportunities for all children.

In reality, our major interests are the non-academic factors: being a good coworker, having perseverance and a good work ethic, the ability to solve problems and think critically. These are skills that will help a person to be successful in college and in the workforce. It stands to reason; therefore, that we must begin to have new conversations about the definition of success. What does it look like? How is it defined? We have to take a look at other aspects of life and education that make students successful, not just formal assessments and grades.

PUTTING THE PIECES TOGETHER

6. **Role of Adults**

   Adults play the most significant role in shaping the minds and spirits of students. The adults in our educational system are there to guide, mold, direct, and redirect the educational ventures and experiences of children. Adults should not be seen merely as supervisors of the teaching and learning process. Rather, they are to be authentic educators who have a moral duty to provide knowledge, skills, good attitudes, and values. Adults must provide educational influences to great life-long learning opportunities for all children. We need to be constantly engaged in the process and present ourselves as learning models for our children.

7. **Role of Qualitative Surveys**

   Qualitative surveys should be conducted as a matter of policy to ensure that schools can develop alternative means of measuring performance. Quality surveys give all the stakeholders: parents, students, and community entities the opportunity to voice their issues, needs and desires, giving feedback on how the school performs. Tangible and authentic reflections provide real feedback on the potential of unintended and purposeful outcomes. Essentially, teachers, students, and stockholders often have a greater buy-in with the implementation of surveys. This is important for addressing perceived needs and the purpose of schooling.

8. **Motivating the Young**

   Motivating learning from a young age is the key determinant in a student's success. Its presence makes the likelihood of achievement greater. Two important strategies to increase motivation are:

a) Creating a warm accepting classroom environment.

b) Creating a model of success, relating schoolwork to students' interests.

Schools and classrooms must help students gain more control over how and when they learn, reinforcing the behavior expected, and highlighting progress within the individual student, instead of comparing their performance with others. Real motivation is intrinsic.

9. The Student's Voice

It goes with saying that the most valued stakeholder is the student, who has the most important say in the educational process. All decisions must be rooted in the best interests of the students and the impact on our culture. Seeing students as the priority and creating environments, where they are included in all decisions, will make a dramatic shift in creating that formula for success. Their insightful options and ideas will create positive changes to facilitate a greater emphasis on learning. As a result, the culture and climate of the school will improve significantly and the priority stakeholder's voice considered – the student.

10. DATE's Contribution to Charter Schools

The current charter schools are models for other entities, both public and private. D.A.T.E has been at the center of exceptional teaching and learning. It has encompassed all of the important factors leading up to the following takeaways:

PUTTING THE PIECES TOGETHER

    a) Understanding the value of all stakeholders' inputs.

    b) Providing substance and relevance in the teaching and learning process.

    c) Challenging students, teachers, and parents with high levels of authentic engagement, while fostering positive and influential relationships.

    d) Understanding the focus and the need to build a community around two pressing issues facing our local as well as the global economy, infrastructure, and family needs: technology and the environment.

    e) Taking a simple yet complex approach to understanding the needs, wants, and desires of learners. This has made it possible to realize the ramifications of putting all the pieces together to produce a quality and substantial product – a top-rated community charter school.

As you continue to apply the lessons shared, some may work and some may not work, but nonetheless, continue to find those puzzle pieces that fit and understand that education is the *key*, and as Nelson Mandela says, "Education is the most powerful weapon which you can use to change the world." Education is the key to eliminating gender inequality, to reducing poverty, to creating a sustainable planet, to preventing needless deaths and illness, and to fostering peace. If we truly want education to be that weapon, as a society, we have to start finding ways that best suit our children, parents, and faculty and staff. These ways are just proven strategies that create that framework for duplicity of success.

ABOUT THE AUTHOR

Dr. Maury Wills is currently the CEO of DeKalb Academy of Technology and Environmental Elementary and Middle Charter Schools, Inc. in suburban Atlanta. Dr. Wills is a native of Austin, Texas.

His skills as an educator and educational administrator have developed throughout a successful career in various fields of education – as a teacher in multiple grades and special education, principal, and special assistant to the superintendent.

With a solid background in educational research and evaluation, Dr. Wills has also served as a consultant to, or member of, numerous educational organizations and initiatives including, Mercer University Educational Study Panel, William Fulbright Scholar Program, Georgia Association of Educators, Association of Curriculum and Instruction, and Association of Supervision and Instruction. He has also received numerous awards and honors including, Extra Mile Award Teacher of the Year, Administrator of the Year, and the Atlanta Constitution and Journal Teacher of the Year nominee.

Dr. Wills was also honored as a William Fulbright Memorial Fund Scholar Recipient having the opportunity to study abroad in Japan. He was only one of two Georgians selected for this prestigious honor in 2001. Recently, Dr. Wills has been invited as a guest lecturer to speak in England on behalf of the charter school movement in America. He has also been featured on several local and national news and radio shows advocating charter schools and their successes.

Dr. Wills' instructional leadership is deeply rooted in his philosophy of excellence and learning: "Every student will learn, given the opportunity to embrace a climate of high expectations, a committed support system, and connections to the context of the real world."

His learning philosophy is based on the three R's: Relationships, Relevance, and Rigor!

Contact Information
Dr. Maury Wills
maurywillsdr@gmail.com

www.ingramcontent.com/pod-product-compliance
Lightning Source LLC
Chambersburg PA
CBHW030332080526
44584CB00012B/832